Sermon Outlines from Acts

Croft M. Pentz

BAKER BOOK HOUSE
Grand Rapids, Michigan

Preface

The Book of Acts is sometimes called "The Works of the Holy Spirit." Starting in chapter two of this book, we see an outpouring of the Spirit. This outpouring took place after ten days of prayer. We see God taking all types of people, filling them with the Holy Spirit and allowing them to do wonders. Peter, who just a short time before had denied Christ, is now a powerhouse for God. We see Saul meeting Christ, and this transformation causes him to be one of the truly great ministers of the Gospel. We see Stephen, a layman, doing great wonders for God. We also see him stoned to death for his faith. This death left a lasting impact upon Saul, who was standing nearby. We see the first church officers, the first hypocrites, and we see the power of God healing many people.

So many wonderful things happened in this book because people allowed the Holy Spirit to work through them. In this outline we have touched on the highlights of the book, realizing that many more lessons could be taken from this great book.

God blessed these outlines as they were given to our people. It was a joy to prepare them and deliver them. My thanks to Mrs. Ella Steinbach who gave her time in typing the manuscript. I also wish to thank the Tyndale House Publishers for allowing me to quote from *The Living Bible*.

We trust that God will bless these outlines and all the people who may use them. May they win many to Christ, as well as establish others in the faith.

—Croft M. Pentz

Copyright 1978 by
Baker Book House Company
ISBN: 0-8010-7039-2

First printing, January 1979
Second printing, October 1980
Third printing, June 1982
Fourth printing, February 1984
Fifth printing, August 1985
Sixth printing, April 1987

Printed in the United States of America

Contents

1

The Lord's Ascension

Acts 1:1-11

The Book of Acts is one of the most thrilling books of the Bible. It is sometimes called the Acts of the Apostles, or the Acts of the Spirit. It shows man praying, witnessing, preaching and teaching. It shows suffering for the Lord. It shows the power of the Holy Spirit working through man. It shows how God poured out His Holy Spirit after Jesus ascended into heaven. We see this power within man as he changes the world.

I. **Divine Proof—vv. 1-3**
   A. Proof—v. 1. Luke refers to his former treatise, the Gospel of Luke. Luke also wrote the entire Book of Acts. Theophilus is an honorary title of people of high sacred and political standing.
   B. Practice—v. 2. This verse refers to Jesus' teachings and His practices and how we, His followers, should continue His work. This is why He told the people to "tarry for power," so they could continue this work—Luke 24:49.
   C. People—v. 3. Christ showed Himself to at least twelve groups of people after He rose from the dead.

II. **Divine Power—vv. 4-8**
   A. Place—v. 4. The 120 people assembled in the upper room in Jerusalem were waiting for the promise of Luke 24:49. They were in no hurry; they prayed for ten days. Remember, there are no short cuts to obtain God's power—it still requires prayer!
   B. Promise—v. 5. John the Baptist baptized with water, but Jesus baptized with the Holy Ghost. The experiences of being baptized with water and being baptized with the Holy Spirit are different from each other.
   C. Perfection—vv. 6-7. The followers of Christ ask a question, "When would Christ set up His kingdom?"—When would He return to earth? Note Jesus' answer in verse 7: No one would know the exact time, except God. See Matthew 24:44.

D. Preaching—v. 8. Power would come to help them witness. Later, this power helped them change the world.

III. Divine Promise—vv. 9–11

A. Ascension—v. 9. Christ ascends into heaven in a cloud.

B. Afraid—v. 10. No doubt the disciples were afraid, since they now would be doing the work of Jesus and facing persecution also.

C. Affirmation—v. 11

 1. Problem—"Why stand ye gazing into heaven?"
 2. Person—"This same Jesus which is taken from you into heaven."
 3. Promise—"Shall come in like manner."

Jesus will come again; He promised to return—John 14:1-3. Paul tells of the manner in which He will come—I Thessalonians 4:13-18. His coming will be unexpected. Note the parable of Matthew 25:1-13. Again and again we see the warning—BE READY! Are you ready? Are you living according to the standards of the Bible? If not, you are not ready to meet Christ. His coming could take place at any moment—be ready!

2

Preparation for Pentecost

Acts 1:12-26

One hundred and twenty people went into the upper room to pray for the promise of Luke 22:49. Both men and women tarried for the promise of power in what could be the same room where Jesus had the Last Supper with the disciples. Jesus had gone to heaven, but His followers would carry on the work He started.

I. **Faithful Apostles—vv. 12–14**
   A. Place—v. 12. The followers of Christ return to Jerusalem after Christ's ascension to pray for power to do His work.
   B. People—v. 13. According to church tradition, this room belonged to John Mark—Acts 12:12. The disciples, with the exception of Judas, were in this group. Judas, who had betrayed Jesus, had committed suicide—Matthew 27:5.
   C. Prayer—v. 14. Both men and women stayed to pray. His "brethren" were the brothers of Jesus. Jesus had four brothers and at least two sisters—Matthew 13:56. Note that Mary, the mother of Jesus, needed the Holy Spirit.

II. **Faithless Apostle—vv. 15–20**
   A. Person—v. 15. Peter, who only a short time before denied the Lord, was now a powerhouse for the Lord.
   B. Prophecy—vv. 16–20
      1. Person—vv. 16–19. Verse 16 refers to Psalm 41:9. Jesus was called to preach, cast out demons and heal the sick. Judas was saved, but fell back into sin. Note: "Judas fell"—Acts 1:25. If he were not a Christian, how could he fall?
      2. Place—v. 20. This is a fulfilment of Psalm 26:23-24, and Psalm 109:8.

III. **Finding an Apostle—vv. 21–26**
   A. Crisis—vv. 21-22. Since Judas "sold" Christ there was a need for someone to take Judas' place.
   B. Characters—v. 23. They select two men, and later they would vote on these.

C. Choice—vv. 24-26
   1. Prayer—vv. 24-25. It is always good to pray before making a choice. Too often human desire is first, and God's choice is not made. Pray for wisdom in your decisions.
   2. Person—v. 26. Matthias is selected to fill Judas' place. From this time on, the disciples are called "the twelve"—Acts 2:1; 6:2.

The followers of Christ were fearful and abandoned Christ in the judgment hall, as well as at the cross. Now we see a change. We will see how this power changes the world. They were now in complete agreement. This attitude shows the proper relationship with God. Opposition to God's work, as well as opposition to His servants, hurts and destroys God's work. The Holy Spirit should unite; He should empower and excite.

3

The Coming of the Holy Spirit

Acts 2:1–8, 12–21

The reason for the growth of the church in the Book of Acts is the Holy Spirit. The Holy Spirit was poured out on the day of Pentecost. This brought excitement and enthusiasm. These people who experienced this happening were filled with power and went out and changed the world. God still gives man this experience. There are no references which say that this experience was for these people only; it is also for today. Those who accept it see a change in their lives.

I. The Might of Pentecost—vv. 1–4
A. Promise—v. 1. The word *pentecost* means fifty, referring to a Jewish feast fifty days after the Passover. People who speak in tongues are called Pentecostal.
B. Power—v. 2. There is a sound from heaven like a rushing mighty wind. It fills the entire house.
C. Personality—v. 3. Cloven tongues, tongues of fire, sat upon all. Jesus would baptize with the Holy Ghost and fire— Matthew 3:11. This fire would cause much excitement!
D. Pentecost—v. 4. The Pentecostal people would establish the first church. They spoke in different languages. The apostle Paul spoke in tongues—I Corinthians 14:18, 14:39.

II. The Marvel of Pentecost—vv. 5–8, 12–15
A. Speaking—vv. 5-6. All types of people were present, including learned Jewish leaders. People from various countries heard these people speak in their native language, a language which the speakers had not learned. See I Corinthians 14:22.
B. Surprise—vv. 1-8. God's Spirit always causes people to ask many questions. These people were speaking to God— I Corinthians 14:2.
C. Sarcastic—v. 13. Some were critical saying, "They are drunk." There has been, and always will be critics. Rather than accept the truth, they have a reason for not accepting it.

D. Spirit—v. 14. These people were not drinking. It was only the third hour, 9:00 a.m. Peter asks that the people listen to his words.

III. **The Meaning of Pentecost—vv. 16–21**
   A. Promise—vv. 16–20. This promise is a fulfillment of Joel 2:28–29, spoken about 800 B.C.
   B. Purpose—v. 21. This is an answer to Acts 1:8. Christ is now in heaven, and the Holy Spirit would empower the followers of Christ to do His work.
   C. Power. This power of the Holy Spirit would help man carry out the great commission—Mark 16:15.

Jesus did not tell people to try to speak in tongues, nor to seek the Holy Spirit. He told them to seek for power. Speaking in tongues is an overflow of the Spirit—John 7:37–39. It brings a deep reverence for God—Acts 2:43, Hebrews 12:28. This promise is for all people—Acts 2:39. It is for all people of all churches. Note Acts 19:2: the people were Christians, but had not received the Holy Spirit.

4

The Results of Pentecost

Acts 2:32-47

On the day of Pentecost, 120 people experienced the baptism of the Holy Spirit (Acts 2:1-4). The learned, as well as the unlearned, spoke in tongues as the Spirit gave them utterance. Peter, who a short time before denied the Lord, now is filled with power and stands before the people explaining this miracle. At the end of his sermon three thousand are converted.

I. **Great Report—vv. 32-36**
   A. Person—v. 32. Jesus was raised from the dead. We are witnesses to this fact. Many saw Christ after His resurrection.
   B. Position—v. 33. Jesus is exalted on the right hand of God. The 120 receive the promise of Luke 24:49.
   C. Proof—vv. 34-35. David, who lived many years before Christ, knew of the coming Messiah. Compare with Psalm 110:1.
   D. Power—v. 36. God made Jesus, the Lord and Christ whom the Jewish people had crucified. Peter tells how the Messiah they were looking for had come, and they had rejected Him.

II. **Great Repentance—vv. 37-41**
   A. Conviction—v. 37. They were convicted and asked, "What must we do?" Prayer brings conviction upon man.
   B. Conversion—v. 38
      1. Repent. The word *repent* simply means to change, or to be sorry enough to quit. Turn around. Live differently.
      2. Be baptized. First repent, then be baptized in water. Baptism does not produce salvation but is a result of salvation.
      3. Receive the gift of the Holy Ghost—the same gift received on the day of Pentecost.
   C. Complete—v. 39. The promise of the Holy Spirit is for people of all ages and generations, as well as all churches.
   D. Change—vv. 40-41
      1. Redemption—v. 40. Change your ways. Be born again—John 3:1-8. Have the experience of II Corinthians 5:17.

2. Results—v. 41. There were three thousand converts—not from Peter's preaching alone but from the ten days of prayer.

III. Great Results—vv. 42-47

A. Faithfulness—v. 42. They continued in the apostles' doctrine and had fellowship in the breaking of bread.

B. Fear—v. 43. They had honor and respect toward God. Signs and wonders and miracles were performed.

C. Fellowship—vv. 44-45. They sold their homes and gave money to the church to help the poor and needy.

D. Firm—vv. 46-47. Note two things: (1) service—they served God daily, (2) soul winning—new converts were added daily.

The people in the Book of Acts had five important things that helped them change their world: (1) Sincere to God—they were serious. (2) Seeking God—they sought divine guidance. (3) Serving God—they served God with all their hearts. (4) Surrendered to God—God had all their hearts, lives and talents. (5) Studied about God—they met in homes, since they had no church buildings to study God's Word.

5
God's Healing Power

Acts 3:1–16

The Holy Spirit produces power: (1) power to work for God, (2) power to worship God, and (3) power to witness for God. Peter and John had God's power in their lives. The power of the Holy Spirit is of little value unless we use it. The crippled man is a picture of the crippled world in need of help from God.

I. **The Prayer for Power—v. 1**
  A. The reason for prayer—Luke 18:1. This is Christ's command: man must take time to pray. Compare with Luke 24:49.
  B. The rule of prayer—Matthew 6:6. Jesus tells of the importance of secret prayer.
  C. The results of prayer—James 5:16. There is no limit to the power of daily, fervent prayer.

II. **The Person in Need of Power—v. 2**
  The world is crippled by the power of sin.
  A. Sin cripples man—Judges 16:20–21. Sin left its mark upon Samson until the day of his death.
  B. Sin controls man—John 8:34. Man becomes a servant and a slave unto sin and Satan.
  C. Sin confuses man—II Corinthians 4:4. Sin blinds both the Christian and the sinner to the truth.

III. **The Power Given to the Person—vv. 3–7**
  A. The plea—"Look upon us." They had something to offer this man. What do you have to offer to the world?
  B. The plan—"What we have we give unto you." They had something real, they had something worthwhile to offer.
  C. The power—"Rise up and walk." They met this man's need through the power of the Holy Spirit. We need the same power.

IV. **The Praising Because of the Power—vv. 8–9**
  A. Leaping. We accept healing by faith in God.

B. Walking. We practice God's healing power by working through Him.

C. Praising. We thank God for the healing.

V. The People Wonder at the Power—vv. 10–11

A. They saw the miracle—v. 10. We should show the world that God can do the impossible by changing lives.

B. They were surprised at the miracle—v. 11. Some accepted this miracle as from God; others rejected it.

VI. The Preaching Which Explains the Power—vv. 12–16

A. Wonder—v. 12. Why wonder? This was God's power at work!

B. Wrong—vv. 13–15. The people reject both the miracle and Christ.

C. Work—v. 16. It was Christ who did this supernatural work.

The world is crippled and needs help. As the church and as Christians we must help. We cannot help the world with our strength alone. We need God's power working in and through us. This power comes only through the power of the Holy Spirit. The Holy Spirit produces supernatural power. To change the heart and lives of man we must have and use this power.

6

Suffering Persecution

Acts 4:1–22

The healing of the crippled man in Acts 3 stirred up the people. They knew Peter had denied Christ, but now he has power. This caused the Jews to punish the Christians. All Christians will suffer persecution—II Timothy 3:12. Note the words of Jesus—Matthew 5:11. Almost all persecution comes from the religious world. The disciples were placed in prison, but they did not stop preaching the gospel.

I. **Divine Power—vv. 1–12**
   A. Persecution—vv. 1–4
      1. Consecration—vv. 1–3. They are dedicated to spreading the gospel.
      2. Conversion—v. 4. Five thousand men were converted.
   B. People—vv. 5–7. The Jewish leaders are interested in how the disciples did these wonderful works.
   C. Power—v. 8. Peter is now a changed man. He is filled with power to explain the miracle—Acts 1:8.
   D. Personality—vv. 9–10
      1. Savior—v. 10. It was Christ who healed the crippled man.
      2. Stone—v. 11. Christ is the cornerstone. See Psalm 118:22, Matt. 21:24.
      3. Salvation—v. 12. Salvation can be realized only through Christ.

II. **Dedicated People—vv. 13–17**
   A. Power—v. 13. Though uneducated, they show the power of God in their lives. Do you show God's power in your life?
   B. Proof—v. 14. The proof of God's power was the healing of the crippled man.
   C. Problem—vv. 15–17
      1. Undeniable—vv. 15–16. They could not deny the miracle of healing the crippled man.
      2. Unstopped—v. 17. The Jewish leaders could not stop the work of God and the dedication of the disciples.

III. Determined People—vv. 19–22

A. Consecration—v. 19. The disciples had to obey God rather than the teachings of man.

B. Challenge—v. 20. The disciples could not remain quiet. They had seen God work in the lives of people. They had a burning in their hearts. See Jeremiah 20:9.

C. Confused—vv. 21–22. The Jewish leaders were confused. They allow the disciples to go free and speak. The disciples could not remain silent.

Many people in the religious world deny God's supernatural power. Some churches are nothing more than religious clubs. Because of this they are not spiritually minded. They do not understand spiritual things. A growing church and a growing Christian will be persecuted and misunderstood. A church or a Christian that is not growing, or not dedicated, receives no persecution or suffering.

7

The First Church

Acts 4:23-37

The disciples were arrested, persecuted and placed in jail for preaching the gospel. They learned to pray together; they worked together and witnessed together. They felt a deep love for each other. Unity was the secret to their success! When there is unity in the church it creates a great power which destroys the power of sin and Satan. The quickest of all ways to destroy the church is disunity. Disunity in the church leads to: (1) division, (2) contention, and (3) confusion.

I. **The People's Consecration—vv. 23-31**
   A. People—v. 23. As soon as the disciples were freed they went to join their own people.
   B. Praise—vv. 24-25. Despite being persecuted they praised the Lord. Verse 25 is part of Psalm 2:1.
   C. Prophecy—vv. 26-28. This is a partial quote of Psalm 2:1-3 showing Christ as Lord, the highest of all and ruler of the world.
   D. Plea—vv. 29-30. The disciples did not pray for freedom but for boldness as they spoke God's Word. They asked that God reach out His hand and heal.
   E. Praying—v. 31. Note the three steps of prayer:
      1. Prayer. The secret to success is prayer.
      2. Place. The place was shaken as the result of prayer.
      3. Power. They spoke God's Word with boldness.

II. **The People's Cooperation—vv. 32-33**
   A. Unusual people—v. 32.
      1. One heart. All had the same feelings toward each other.
      2. One soul. All had the same spiritual desires.
      3. One desire. They shared what they had with others.

III. **The People's Compassion—vv. 34-37**
   A. Sameness—v. 34. The people sold their houses and shared their money with other poor Christians. This was before they had welfare or social security.

B. Sharing—v. 35. The people sold their homes and gave the money to the disciples, and the disciples gave it to those in need.

C. Surrender—v. 36. Barnabas sold his land and gave the money to the disciples.

Should Christians sell their homes and give the money to the church? The Bible says that first we should take care of our families—Galatians 6:10, James 2:15-16. We should pay our tithes—Malachi 3:8-19. God may ask us if we *are willing* to surrender everything to Him. We should obey Him no matter what He may tell us to do. God wants to be first in our lives.

8

Hypocrites in the Church

Acts 5:1–4, 11–16

The early church was made a success because of faith, purpose and service. Barnabas set a good example for the people. However, not every one followed his example. Unbelief and carnal living hinders God's work from going forward. Such living hurts not only God's work but discourages man. In this passage we see a husband and wife—Ananias and Sapphira—lying not to man but to God. As the result of their lying God struck them dead.

I. **Hypocrisy Perpetrated—vv. 1–2**
   A. The people—v. 1. Ananias and Sapphira sold their possessions with the thought in mind of giving the money to the church. They were following the example of Barnabas.
   B. The problem—v. 2. They kept back part of the money though they had promised to give it all. By breaking this promise they lied to God! Never make a promise you cannot keep!

II. **Hypocrisy Perceived—vv. 3–4**
   A. Satan—v. 3. Satan tempted Ananias and Sapphira to lie to God. God revealed to Peter that they were lying. Note these biblical statements about lying:
      1. Satan is the father of lies—John 8:44.
      2. God hates a lying tongue—Proverbs 6:17.
      3. All unforgiven liars will go to hell—Revelation 21:8.
   B. Sin—v. 4. All lying is sin. These people lied to God. It is never right to tell a lie.

   There are many ways in which a person may lie:
      1. Double living—Luke 6:46.
      2. Being a hypocrite—1 John 1:6.
      3. Blaming others for your faults and failures.
      4. Stretching the truth is also lying.

III. **Hypocrisy Punished—vv. 11–16**
   A. Problem—v. 11. Fear came upon the people. God's judgment always brings fear and respect.

B. Power—v. 12. Many signs and wonders were done. Note: "They were all with one accord." The unity of spirit and purpose brought about these miracles.
C. People—vv. 13-14. In verse 13, the unbelievers could not stand in the presence of God. In verse 14, many were converted unto Christ.
D. Perfection—vv. 15-16. Peter was so filled with God's power that even his shadow healed the people. God is interested in the whole man—soul, body, mind.

The church cannot grow when there is sin in the church. Note the words of Peter: "And if the righteous scarcely be saved, where shall the ungodly and the sinner appear"—I Peter 4:18. The Scripture teaches that judgment must begin at the house of God—I Peter 4:17. When Christians live right, sinners will be converted.

9

Divine Deliverance

Acts 5:17-42

The death of Ananias and Sapphira didn't seem to change the Jewish leaders. Their attitude remained the same toward the Christians. As the followers of Christ continued to spread the gospel, the Jewish leaders became angry. They did all in their power to destroy Christianity. No one can destroy God's work—Matthew 16:18.

I. **The Testing of the Apostles—vv. 17–26**
   A. Problem—vv. 17–18. The Jewish leaders were jealous of the Christians. The High Priest and the Sadducees put the disciples into prison for preaching.
   B. Preaching—vv. 19–20. An angel came and freed these twelve men from prison. They were told to go forth and preach again.
   C. Planning—v. 21. The Jewish leaders called the council and met in the Sanhedrin court to decide what to do with these people.
   D. Power—vv. 23–24. The disciples had miraculously escaped with the gates closed and the guards standing on duty.
   E. People—vv. 25–26
      1. The high priest doubted their escape from prison.
      2. The apostles were busy preaching and teaching in the temple.
      3. The captains and officers brought the disciples before the council. They feared these Christians.

II. **The Testimony of the Apostles—vv. 27–32**
   A. Command—vv. 27–28. The disciples were warned not to preach again. Note: they filled Jerusalem with their doctrine.
   B. Concern—v. 29. Obey God first, then obey man. All Christians should obey the laws of the city, state and nation. However, if these laws keep us from serving God, then we should not keep them.
   C. Cleansing—vv. 30–31. Christ's death upon the cross cleanses us from all sin. See I John 1:7, Psalm 103:3.

D. Consecration—v. 32. The apostles were witnesses of these many things, as well as witnesses of the Holy Spirit.

III. **The Triumph of the Apostles—vv. 33–42**
   A. Anger—v. 33. The preaching of God's Word brings anger to the unbeliever. God's Word always brings conviction to the believer.
   B. Attitude—v. 34–39. Gamaliel, a very wise man, tells the Jewish leaders not to harm the apostles. If what the apostles were preaching was of God, they would be fighting against God.
   C. Affliction—v. 40. The apostles were freed after being beaten. Compare with II Timothy 3:12.
   D. Affection—vv. 41–42
      1. Love for suffering—v. 41. It is counted a joy to suffer for Him.
      2. Love for service—v. 42. In the temple they preached God's Word daily.

The apostles had a fire that burned within them. The prisons and beatings could not stop them. Jeremiah had this same fire—Jeremiah 20:9. A fire of God in the heart will send us out to witness and win others unto the Lord. We enjoy God's blessings today because many were willing to suffer for the sake of the Lord. Are we willing to do the same?

10

The First Church Officers

Acts 6:1-7; I Peter 5:1-10

The Holy Spirit guided the early church. This guidance helped them overcome their problems and taught them to accept persecution willingly. As the church grew there were problems. Always remember that growth brings changes, as well as problems. The Holy Spirit united the people, and they cooperated in solving the problems and making the church grow.

I. **The Problems in the Church—Acts 6:1**
   A. Success of the church. God caused the church to grow and prosper in every way. He will do this to all churches, if He is invited.
   B. Sarcasm in the church. There was a murmuring of the Grecians against the Hebrews. There are always those, including Christians, who always complain about any change in the church.
   C. Selfishness in the church. The widows were neglected. Of course, there was no social security or welfare at this time.

II. **The Plan of the Church—Acts 6:2-7**
   A. Problem—v. 2. The disciples didn't want to do the work the laymen could do. Too often a pastor is overloaded with work.
   B. Plea—v. 3. They select seven men to assist the apostles in the church. Note the requirements of these men:
      1. Christian men—"look among you." They wanted born-again Christians.
      2. Spiritual men—"full of the Holy Ghost." They wanted men who had not only experienced the Holy Ghost—Acts 2:4, but who also demonstrated the fruits of their experience—Galatians 5:22-23.
      3. Wise men. They wanted mature, experienced men.
   C. Prayer—v. 4. Notice the two-fold ministry of the disciples.
      1. Prayer.
      2. Ministry of the Word.
   D. People—vv. 5-6. The seven men were chosen. The apostles blessed them and sent them out to work for Christ.

E. Power—v. 7. They increased in power as they were obedient and faithful.

III. **The Personality of the Church—I Peter 5:1–10**

A. Sacred—vv. 1–3. Some leaders fall into sin and become poor examples. Peter gives the example for the leaders.

B. Shepherd—v. 4. Christ, the chief Shepherd, shall appear and shall reward us for all our faithfulness.

C. Submission—v. 5. Younger Christians should respect and submit to older Christian people. Note: "clothed with humility."

D. Surrender—v. 6. Be humble. Have self discipline. Don't praise yourself. Allow others to praise you.

E. Solace—v. 7. 'Cast all your care upon Him, since He cares for you.' All troubles, problems and sorrows should be cast upon Him.

F. Sober—v. 8. Wake up! Watch out! Be careful about Satan!

G. Suffering—v. 9. Be firm and strong like a rock!

H. Strength—v. 10. Note: (1) suffer, (2) make you perfect. (3) stablish, (4) strengthen you, and (5) settle you.

God seeks men and women who will do His work. He seeks people who are willing to work long hard hours; people who will surrender their time as well as money to the Lord; people who will work when others refuse to. Such people will be used by God and will bring blessing to many. They will help the church to grow and be a success.

11

Stephen the Martyr

Acts 6:8–15; 7:1–2, 8–9, 22–25, 37, 54–60

The power of Pentecost spread to all people. When they prayed, they prayed with power—Acts 4:31. As they used this power the church grew. The more the church grew, the more they faced persecution. The Jewish leaders tried to scare God's people by using Stephen as an example. He was stoned and killed before the other Christians. However, this did not stop the Christians.

I. **The Trial of Stephen—6:8–15**
   A. Person—v. 8. Stephen was a layman. He was one of the seven men chosen to help the apostles—Acts 6:5. The Holy Spirit worked through him, performing many wonders and miracles.
   B. Problem—v. 9. These wonders stirred up the non-Christians. When God works the sinner is offended and disturbed.
   C. Power—v. 10. The non-Christians could not resist the wisdom which Stephen displayed as he spoke.
   D. People—vv. 11–12. The leaders helped to stir up the people to oppose Stephen and the other Christians. Stephen was wrongly accused. He was brought before the council.
   E. Perversion—vv. 13–14. The leaders had false witnesses speak against Stephen. These people did not know the full truth.
   F. Purity—v. 15. Stephen's face shone, just as Moses' face shone—Exodus 34:29–35.

II. **The Testimony of Stephen—7:1–2, 8–9, 22–25, 37**
   A. Divine purpose—vv. 1–2. God led Abraham to Charan (Haran), 420 miles north of Jerusalem. He wants to lead you in your daily life.
   B. Divine promise—v. 8. God's promise or covenant to Abraham signals the start of the twelve tribes. All fit into God's plan.
   C. Divine protection—v. 9. Though Joseph's brothers sold him, yet God protected him to preserve the Jewish race. Though the New Testament was not yet written, Joseph knew the meaning of Romans 8:28.

D. Divine pity—vv. 22–25. Moses felt sorry for his people; then he became their leader.

E. Divine prophet—v. 37. Moses is speaking here of the coming of Christ.

III. The Triumph of Stephen—7:54–60

A. Problem—v. 54. These leaders didn't want to know the truth. As the result of this attitude they became angry.

B. Power—vv. 55–56

1. Spirit—v. 55. He was full of the Holy Spirit. This is the secret of success.

2. Satisfaction—v. 56. Jesus is standing to welcome Stephen at the right hand of God. See Matthew 26:64, Ephesians 1:20.

C. Persecution—vv. 57–58. The people became angry and cast Stephen out of the city. His clothes were laid at the feet of Saul.

D. Prayer—vv. 59–60. As he dies he prays for his enemies.

The Jewish leaders felt that killing Stephen would destroy Christianity. Saul watches him die, and later becomes one of the great preachers. The death of Stephen left an impact upon Saul which he could not forget. Stephen was willing to suffer for the Lord.

12

Outreach of the Church

Acts 8:1–24

The Jewish leaders had Stephen stoned to death. The more they persecuted the Christians, the more the church grew. The fire of the Holy Spirit could not be put out. The prophet Jeremiah had this burning in his bones—Jeremiah 20:9. This persecution caused the Christians to be spread to the surrounding cities, preaching the gospel wherever they went.

I. **The Persecution—vv. 1–4**
  A. Persecutor—v. 1. Saul was pleased with the death of Stephen. As the result of this persecution, the church was scattered.
  B. Pity—v. 2. The friends of Stephen mourned for him. They also had a funeral for him.
  C. Persecution—v. 3. Saul enjoyed the persecution of the Christians. The persecution made the Christians stronger in the Lord.
  D. Preaching—v. 4. This persecution caused the Christians to go everywhere preaching the gospel. The promise of Mark 16:18 was fulfilled.

II. **The Preaching—vv. 5–13**
  A. Person—v. 5. Philip preached of Jesus—no politics, no social gospel, no civil rights, but of Jesus!
  B. People—v. 6. The people "gave heed" to Philip's words and the many miracles which were done in the name of the Lord.
  C. Power—v. 7. The people who were bound by Satan were set free. Various types of sickness were healed by God's power.
  D. Peace—v. 8. There was great joy in the city.
  E. Problem—vv. 9–11. Simon used witchcraft to deceive people.
  F. Purging—vv. 12–13. Many people believed.

III. **The Prayer—vv. 14–17**
  A. Sent—vv. 14–15. The apostles sent John and Peter to Samaria. They prayed that the people might receive the Holy Spirit.

B. Spirit—vv. 16-17
   1. Realization—v. 16. They had not yet received the Holy Spirit. They were baptized in water, but not the Holy Spirit.
   2. Reception—v. 17. Peter and John laid hands on them, and they received the Holy Spirit.

IV. The Problem—vv. 18-24
A. Desire—vv. 18-19. Simon saw the power of the Holy Spirit and wanted it for selfish gain. He offered money for this gift.
B. Denouncement—vv. 20-23. Peter showed him his wrong, that money could not buy this power, and warned him to repent of his sin.
C. Damnation—v. 24. Simon asked for prayer. We do not know if he repented of his sin or not.

Simon's temptation is still with us today. Many seek God's power for personal benefit and spiritual pride. Any gift or talent God may give to us is for advancement of the kingdom of God. Never should we use the power of God for selfish gain. Some Christians boast of their praying, Bible reading and generosity.

13

Personal Witnessing

Acts 8:26–40

There are various ways of evangelizing. The best method is personal soul-winning. This means work; it means visitation. This is the hardest way to reach man with the gospel. If this method would be followed by Christians, we could easily change the world. The next method is through the church. Other methods are church literature and mass meetings. Philip left a large crowd to win *one* soul.

I. **The Spirit—vv. 26–29**
   A. Person—v. 26. Philip was one of the seven men chosen by the apostles. He had a revival in Samaria. An angel spoke to him and told him to go to another place.
   B. Problem—v. 27. An Ethiopian or a eunuch, a man of great power and influence, came to Jerusalem seeking the Lord.
   C. Prophecy—v. 28. This man was reading from Isaiah, the prophet. The New Testament was not yet completed.
   D. Plea—v. 29. The Holy Spirit tells Philip to go to the chariot of this eunuch. Be open; allow God to speak to you.

II. **The Speaking—vv. 30–35**
   A. Problem—vv. 30–31. Philip was quick to obey God; he ran to the eunuch, who was reading from Isaiah, but could not understand what he was reading. Compare with Romans 10:14.
   B. Prophecy—vv. 32–33. He was reading from Isaiah 53:7–8. This was a prophecy concerning Christ, who would come to save man from sin.
   C. Plight—v. 34. The eunuch asked, "Who is the Prophet speaking about?" The non-Christian is in darkness; he needs help.
   D. Preaching—v. 35. Notice that Philip preached about Jesus. He told him all about Jesus.

III. **The Salvation—vv. 36–40**
   A. Salvation—v. 36. The eunuch understood and accepted Christ. He wanted to be baptized. See Acts 2:38.

B. Sincere—v. 37. Philip wanted to be sure the eunuch understood water baptism, before he baptized him.
C. Showing—v. 38. Philip went down into the water with the eunuch and baptized him. Water baptism is an outward sign of salvation.
D. Spirit—vv. 39-40. The Spirit took Philip approximately twenty-five miles away from the eunuch. Philip stayed in the Caesara area for twenty-five years—Acts 21:8-9. His daughters were filled with the Holy Spirit and used the gift of prophecy.

All men are sinners—Romans 3:23. Though all men are sinners most do not know this, nor do they know how to have this sin removed. There is only one way they can know about forgiveness—they must be told. If each layman does his part in witnessing, soon all will know. God could work through angels, but He depends upon man—John 15:16. Every Christian should be a personal soul-winner. God gives us power to do this work—Acts 1:8.

14

Supernatural Power

Acts 9:32–43

The ministry of Christ was a miracle ministry. He came to destroy the works of the devil. He came to overcome sin and sickness. He showed a concern for both the soul and the body. He still performs miracles; salvation is a miracle—John 3:18, II Corinthians 5:17. Paul spoke of people having a form of godliness, but denying its power—II Timothy 3:5. Jesus promised signs and wonders—Mark 16:20, Matthew 28:20.

I. **The Power—vv. 32–35**
   A. People—v. 32. Peter comes to the saints at Lydda. *Saints* are people, born-again by the power of God. Lydda was twenty-three miles northeast of Jerusalem.
   B. Problem—v. 33. Aeneas was sick with palsy for eight years.
   C. Perfection—v. 34. Peter tells Aeneas to be healed in the name of Jesus. He arose and was healed. See Philippians 2:10–11.
   D. Power—v. 35. All the people in Saron, where Lydda was located, turned unto the Lord. This healing took place to bring honor and glory to God. God does heal today. Healing was provided by Christ on the cross—Isaiah 53:5, I Peter 2:24. See also III John 2.

II. **The Problem—vv. 36–41**
   A. Person—v. 36. Dorcas who lived in Joppa was filled with good works. Joppa was a seaport about thirty-five miles northeast of Jerusalem.
   B. Problem—v. 37. Dorcas becomes ill and dies.
   C. People—vv. 38–39. Two men visit Peter and ask him to come to Joppa. Peter leaves Lydda and goes to Joppa.
   D. Prayer—v. 40. Peter stays alone in the room with Dorcas, praying for her.
   E. Power—v. 41. Dorcas comes to life through Peter's prayer.

III. **The Publicity—vv. 42–43**
   A. Results—v. 42. Dorcas went back to the work of helping

people after she came to life. Many people saw it, and many believed.

1. God's power convicts men of their sin.
2. God's power convinces men to give up their sin.
3. God's power converts men from their sin.

   B. Residence—v. 43. Peter remained in the city for many days with Simon, the tanner.

God gives His power to man for a purpose. His power is given that it may be used to bring honor and glory unto the Lord. There are those whom God blesses who misuse His power, and even become proud of the works they perform. As the result of this, they lose God's power from their lives. We should pray and expect God to do great things through our lives—Jeremiah 33:3, Ephesians 3:20.

15

Peter Preaches to the Gentiles

Acts 10:1-5, 9-15, 27-28, 34-38, 44-48; 11:1-2, 17-19

The promise of the Holy Spirit in Acts 1:8 was four-fold: (1) to Jerusalem, (2) to Samaria, (3) to Judea, (4) to the uttermost parts of the world. At one time only the Jews were hearing the gospel. Since the Gentiles were enemies of the Jews, they were not given the gospel after the day of Pentecost. The gospel is for all people—John 3:16, Romans 10:13. Peter was the first to bring the gospel to the Gentiles.

I. The People—10:1-5, 9-15
   A. Dedication—vv. 1-2. Cornelius was, "a devout man and one that feared God . . . gave much alms . . . and prayed to God alway."
   B. Dream—vv. 3-5. Cornelius had a vision at the ninth hour (3:00 P.M.). God tells him to go to Joppa to see Peter.
   C. Detained—vv. 9-15. As Peter prayed on the house top a large sheet of animals came down. Peter was told to eat, but refused, feeling they were unclean. What God has cleaned is not unclean or common—v. 15.

II. The Plan—10:19-20, 27-28
   A. Spirit—v. 19. The Holy Spirit speaks to Peter.
   B. Sent—v. 20. The Holy Spirit sends Peter to meet two people. God had also sent these men to meet Peter.
   C. Sincere—vv. 25-27. When Cornelius saw Peter coming he bowed before Peter. Peter tells him to stand up—he was a man, not God.
   D. Showing—v. 28. God shows that all people are equal with Him.

III. The Preaching—10:34-38
   A. People—v. 34. God has no favorites. All are the same in His sight. He loves all the same.
   B. Plan—v. 35. All the people who fear or respect God are accepted by Him.

C. Person—vv. 36-38. Christianity was preached to the entire area and many accepted.

IV. The Power—vv. 44-48
A. Preaching—v. 44. As Peter speaks the Holy Spirit falls.
B. People—vv. 45-47. The Gentiles receive the Holy Spirit and are baptized in water.
C. Plea—v. 48. The people ask Peter to remain with them.

V. The Prejudice—11:1-2, 17-19
A. Prejudice—vv. 1-2. Prejudice means to be narrowminded—making up your mind without having all the facts.
B. Peace—vv. 17-19. After hearing what God was doing among the Gentiles, the Jews rejoice with Peter and others of God's blessings among the Gentiles.

The gospel is for all people. Some would like to keep the gospel to their own small group. They enjoy hearing God's Word from their pastor, but have no concern for those outside the church without Christ. As long as they hear the gospel they are satisfied. The church must reach out to all people.

16

The First Christians

Acts 11:19-30

After Stephen's death the Christians were scattered. As they spread out they preached the gospel. The Holy Spirit filled these people with the fire of God. This was the same fire that Jeremiah had burning in his bones—Jeremiah 20:9. More and more Gentiles heard the gospel and as the result, the great commission of Christ (Mark 16:15) was being fulfilled.

I. The Preaching—vv. 19–21
    A. Persecution—v. 19. As persecution came the Christians were scattered and as the result, the people at Antioch heard the gospel. The Christian will always face persecution!
    B. Preaching—v. 20. They preached to the Greeks of the Lord Jesus Christ.
    C. Power—v. 21. The Lord was with them. A good number believed and accepted the Lord.

II. The Person—vv. 22–26
    A. Sending—v. 22. The Christians at Jerusalem sent Barnabas from Jerusalem to Antioch. The church at Jerusalem was interested in what was happening at Antioch.
    B. Satisfaction—v. 23. When Barnabas saw what was happening he was happy and exhorted the people to live for God regardless of the price. Note the price: II Timothy 3:12, Luke 9:23.
    C. Spirituality—v. 24. Note the character of Barnabas: he was a good man, full of the Holy Ghost and of faith. As the result of the work of Barnabas, "Much people were added unto the Lord."
    D. Showing—vv. 25-26. Barnabas remained in Antioch about one year. The non-Christians at Antioch saw the followers of Christ living a Christian life, and the non-Christians called these followers of Christ—*Christians*.

III. The Passion—vv. 27–30
    A. Prophets—v. 27. Some of the prophets came from Jeruslem to Antioch.

B. Prophecy—v. 28. They foretold of a coming famine which would take place in that area.

C. Passion—v. 29. All the followers of Christ gave help to those in need. Every person gave "according to his ability."

Giving shows true Christianity and is a good test of spirituality. The word *Christian* is used in the wrong way many times. Often people say, "If you are not Jewish, then you are Christian." What is a Christian? To be in the Christian family, you must be born into it—John 3:1-8. After you are in the Christian family you follow the teachings of the Bible.

17

Deliverance by a Miracle

Acts 12:1-17

The strong Christian accepts persecution and punishment gladly. The weak Christian resents this and sometimes falls away from God because he cannot stand persecution. No one can be a successful Christian without suffering for the Lord. Note the words of Paul—II Timothy 3:12. Note also the words of Jesus—John 15:18-19.

I. **Punishment for Peter—vv. 1-4**
   A. Persecution—v. 1. Herod began to persecute Christians. Christianity grows the fastest when under persecution.
   B. Punishment—vv. 2-3. James is killed. Herod sees how it pleases the people, so he places Peter in prison.
   C. Prison—v. 4. Though Peter was in prison, Herod could not imprison the power of God. In the Book of Acts the more the people suffered, the more the church grew.

II. **Prayer for Peter—vv. 5-6**
   A. Peter's fate—v. 5a. Herod had planned to have Peter killed.
   B. Peter's friends—v. 5b
      1. Unceasing prayer—II Thessalonians 5:17. The church remained in an attitude of prayer for Peter.
      2. Unfainting prayer—Luke 18:1. Never give up. Though we may not see an answer to our prayers we must keep praying.
      3. Unlimited power—James 5:16. There is no limit to the power of prayer. It changes people, things and circumstances.
   C. Peter's faith—v. 6. Though in prison and bound with chains, yet Peter was sleeping. What faith! Perhaps he knew Philippians 4:7.

III. **Peter in Prison—vv. 7-11**
   A. Divine provision—vv. 7-8
      1. Freedom—v. 7. The chains are loosed; he is set free!
      2. Following—v. 8. Peter is told to follow the angel.
   B. Divine power—vv. 9-11. At first Peter thought he was dreaming. Now he knows it is God's power that is setting him free.

IV. Power of Prayer—vv. 12–17

    A. Freedom—v. 12. Peter visits the home where the people are praying for him. The Bible says we should pray for one another—Galatians 6:2. We should help bear other people's burdens.

    B. Faithless—vv. 13–16. Rhoda hears Peter's voice at the door. Those who were praying didn't believe her.

    C. Favor—v. 17. It pleased God to free Peter and show His power over the forces of man.

God freed Peter, but James was killed and John was beheaded. Some people God delivers; others he permits to suffer and die. All the disciples with the exception of John faced death by the non-Christians. Paul had scars upon his body for the sake of the gospel—Galatians 6:17. Do you love Christ enough to die for Him? If a person cannot live for God, then they could never die for Him.

18

A Church Problem

Acts 15:1–20

To the Jews the Old Testament law was more important than love; good works and good deeds were more important than the grace of God. Many of the Jewish laws were ceremonial laws and were applicable for a certain time. We are not expected to follow these ceremonial laws today (I Timothy 4:4–5).

I. **The Problem—vv. 1–5**
  A. The dilemma—v. 1. The Jewish ceremonial law did not apply to the people of the New Testament.
  B. The discussion—v. 2. Paul and Barnabas discuss the matter with the Jews. Later, they talk to the apostles also.
  C. The delight—v. 3. They rejoice because the Gentiles were converted—without keeping the Jewish ceremonial law. Note the words of Paul—Romans 1:16.
  D. The description—v. 4. Paul and Barnabas explain God's blessing of their ministry. God's Word always produces results.
  E. The demand—v. 5. The laws of the Jewish nation were not the way of salvation. Compare with Ephesians 2:8–9.

II. **The Particulars—vv. 6–12**
  A. The people—v. 6. The apostles and church elders meet to decide the problem concerning the salvation of the Gentiles.
  B. The preaching—vv. 7–11.
    1. The choice—v. 7. God chooses Peter to preach to the Gentiles. Keep in mind, the gospel is for all people—John 3:16.
    2. The confirmation—vv. 8–9. God accepts people of all races who repent of their sin—Romans 10:13.
    3. The confusion—vv. 10–11. The people could be saved without accepting the Jewish ceremonial law.
  C. The power—v. 12. The testimony of the converts was enough proof that they did not need the Jewish laws. See II Corinthians 5:17.

III. The Plan—vv. 13-20

A. The person—vv. 13-14. Saving the Gentiles brought honor and glory to God. At first only the Jews had the gospel.

B. The prophecy—vv. 15-17. The prophecy of Amos 9:11-12 is fulfilled. The truth of the Bible is proven when prophecies are fulfilled.

C. The purpose—v. 18. It was God's plan from the start that all men would be saved. Jesus suffered for the sins of us all—Isaiah 53:6.

D. The plan—vv. 19-20. Since the Gentiles were converted it was not necessary to follow the Jewish ceremonial laws. When one is converted he follows the laws of the Bible.

God loves all people and all races. A converted person should also love all people. This love is not based on the color of the skin, where a person lives or how much money he has. We should look upon the real person. If we love God we will keep His commands, and one of His commands is to 'love others as we love ourselves.'

19

Punishment and Pardon

Acts 16:14–33

Salvation always leads to suffering. It could be persecution from the non-Christian. It could be mental suffering: your family and friends do not understand, and you suffer mentally. Note the words of Jesus in John 15:18–19. The suffering of Paul and Silas gives us an excellent example to follow when we are persecuted for the sake of the Lord.

I. The People—vv. 14–18
  A. Salvation—vv. 14–15. Lydia becomes a Christian.
  B. Satanic—vv. 16–17. Satan controls this woman. She has Satanic power to understand the future.
  C. Supernatural—v. 18. Paul casts Satan out of the woman. Note that this power is given to Christians—Mark 16:17.

II. The Punishment—vv. 19–24
  A. Plan—v. 19. The demon is gone. Paul and Silas are brought before the leaders.
  B. Punishment—vv. 20–24
    1. Plan—vv. 20–21. Lies are told; Paul and Silas are accused of teaching a false religion.
    2. Pain—vv. 22–23. They are whipped with thirty-nine lashes.
    3. Prisoners—v. 24. Not only are they placed in prison, but in stocks as well.

III. The Praise—v. 25
  A. Inner praise. The joy of the Lord was within them.
  B. Outward praise. What is inside of us will soon show in our behavior. A person cannot keep the joy of the Lord within.

IV. The Power—vv. 26–29
  A. Freedom—v. 26. The earthquake opened the doors of the prison, and the prisoners could have escaped.
  B. Fear—v. 27. The prison keeper, thinking that the prisoners had escaped, was planning to commit suicide.

C. Faith—vv. 28–29. Paul tells the prison keeper not to kill himself. No one had escaped from the prison.

V. **The Pardon—vv. 30–33**
  A. Searching—v. 30. The prison keeper asks the question, "What must I do to be saved?"
  B. Salvation—v. 31
    1. Faith. "Believe in the Lord Jesus Christ."
    2. Forgiveness. "And thou shalt be saved."
    3. Family. "And thy house."
  C. Surrender—vv. 32–33. The prison keeper was saved, and his family was baptized in water.

Paul and Silas did not preach a sermon to the prison keeper. They showed the joy of the Lord. They could not remain silent; something burned within their hearts. People will be impressed with your actions—not your words. How you live and act under pressure is important.

20

Paul Preaches Christ

Acts 17:1-14

Paul and the other Christians in the Book of Acts were so filled with the power of God that they could not remain quiet! Everywhere they went they preached the gospel. In prison, before rulers, in the Jewish temple, they told of God's saving power. This preaching stirred up the non-Christian. Persecution always comes when God's Word is preached. But the persecution didn't stop these Christians.

I. **The Opportunity—vv. 1–4.**
   A. Place—v. 1. Thessalonica. Paul later wrote a letter to the people at Thessalonica. They passed through Appollonia (belonging to the sun god, Apollo).
   B. Practice—v. 2. Paul's custom for three Sabbaths was to reason with them from the Scriptures.
   C. Plan—v. 3. God's plan: (1) the suffering of Christ, (2) His resurrection, (3) Jesus the Christ (man's only hope)—John 14:6.
   D. Pardon—v. 4. Many accept Christ and follow Paul in the way of the Savior.

II. **The Opposition—vv. 5–9**
   A. Plan—v. 5. The authorities planned to assault and punish them before the people. The Bible tells of this suffering for the sake of the Lord—John 15:18-19, II Timothy 3:12.
   B. Power—vv. 6-7
      1. Witnessing power—v. 6. They changed their world. They did this without church buildings, printed Bibles, gospel literature, trains, buses, TV or radio.
      2. Worshiping power—v. 7. They didn't worship Caesar, but the Lord. They put Christ first—Matthew 6:33.
   C. People—vv. 8-9. The people of the city were troubled. When Paul promised he wouldn't come back they let him go free.

III. **The Openness—vv. 10–14**
   A. Released—v. 10. Paul and Silas were released at night.

B. Reception—vv. 11-12. The Greeks and others received God's Word of salvation with readiness of mind.
C. Results—vv. 13-14. The Jewish leaders incited the people to oppose the gospel. Should the people accept this opposition to the gospel, they would find how wrong the Jewish teachings really were.

Paul and others suffered greatly for the Lord. They were persecuted and mistreated, but instead of giving up Christ they became stronger in the Lord. Remember, the same sun that softens the clay will also harden the clay. Persecution drives some people away from God, while it brings others to the Lord. To be an effective Christian will mean persecution and misunderstanding.

21

The Unknown God

Acts 17:22-34

Athens was one place where Paul preached where there was not an established church. Most of the Athenians were too proud to admit they were sinners and needed Christ as Savior. Note the words of Paul: "For the preaching of the cross is to them that perish foolishness; but unto us which are saved it is the power of God"—I Corinthians 1:18. The people didn't know God because of ignorance and rejection.

I. **The Ignorant People—vv. 22-23**
   A. Superstition—v. 22. There is no such thing as good or bad luck. The Christian believes that God has a reason or purpose for all things—Romans 8:28. Rabbit's feet, horse shoes and good luck pieces will not change fate.
   B. Sacrilege—v. 23
      1. Idol worship. The Ten Commandments forbid idol worship—Exodus 20:1-5. We should worship God, and Him alone.
      2. Ignorant worship. The altar bore an inscription to "the unknown god." We can know the true God in a personal way—II Timothy 1:12.

II. **The Infinite Power—vv. 24-28**
   A. God's power—v. 24. He made the world—John 1:3. He is Lord of heaven and earth. He is over all; He controls all.
   B. God's personality—v. 25. Do not worship Him with idols made of hands. Idols are lifeless. God gives life and breath.
   C. God's purpose—vv. 26-27
      1. Nationality—v. 26. Under God we are one blood and one nation. God does not look upon the color of skin or upon nationality.
      2. Nearness—v. 27. God is as near as a prayer.
   D. God's plan—v. 28. "For in him we live and move and are! As one of your poets says, 'We are the Sons of God' "—LB. Compare with John 1:12.

44

III. The Impending Punishment—vv. 29–34

    A. Reasoning—v. 29. God is not an idol made by the hands of man! The Trinity (Father, Son and Holy Spirit) had no beginning and will have no end.

    B. Repentance—v. 30. The past ignorance is forgotten. Now all men should repent. Note the words of Jesus—Luke 13:3.

    C. Righteousness—v. 31. Judgment day will come for sinners—Hebrew 9:27, Revelation 20:11–15. There will be a different judgment for Christians—II Corinthians 5:10, Romans 14:10–12.

    D. Resurrection—vv. 32–34. Some wanted to hear more, but others rejected the resurrection.

Today man has no real excuse for not knowing the Lord. Man has a choice, either to accept or reject the Lord. If he believes he will be saved; if he rejects God he will be lost—Mark 16:16. Those who hear the gospel often and reject it will receive more punishment than those who hear it only once and reject it. God is alive; He is real. We can know Him in a personal way.

22

Paul Preaches at Corinth

Acts 18:1-11, I Corinthians 2:1-5

Paul goes to Corinth which was a large metropolitan area. This area was like all other large cities—filled with sin and with no desire to know or seek God. Paul did not go to impress people with his speaking ability; he went to win them to Christ. He preached the gospel. He didn't preach a social gospel, civil rights or reform; he preached Christ.

I. **Fellowship in Christ—Acts 18:1-4**
   A. Place—v. 1. Corinth. Later, Paul wrote two letters to the Christians in this city.
   B. People—v. 2. Some feel these people were already Christians and were serving the Lord.
   C. Practice—v. 3. Paul worked as a tentmaker to support himself. Later, he said, "In the same way the Lord has given orders that those who preach the Gospel should be supported by those who accept it"—I Corinthians 9:14, LB. ". . . Christian workers should be paid by those they help"—I Corinthians 9:10. See also Luke 10:7.
   D. Preaching—v. 4. Paul ministered to both the Jews and the Greeks. He fulfilled Mark 16:15.

II. **Faithfulness in Christ—Acts 18:5-11**
   A. Sorrow—v. 5. Paul was "pressed in the spirit." He preached to the Jews that Christ was the promised Messiah.
   B. Stubborn—v. 6. Paul leaves the Jews because they reject his message. He followed Jesus' words—Matthew 10:14.
   C. Salvation—vv. 7-8. The Corinthians accepted Paul's words. They were converted and were baptized. They believed Romans 10:9-10.
   D. Speaking—v. 9. The Lord tells Paul not to be afraid to speak God's Word—See Romans 10:17, Hebrews 4:12.

III. **Faith in Christ—I Corinthians 2:1-5**
   A. Simplicity—v. 1. Paul advises them not to try to impress, but to make it simple for all to understand. Note these words: "He

tells us everything over and over again, a line at a time and in such simple words."—Isaiah 28:10, LB.
  B. Savior—v. 2. Paul wanted to know one thing: he wanted to know Christ—Philippians 3:10. He had no desire for fame or riches.
  C. Shyness—v. 3. Note Paul's character: he was weak, fearful and filled with trembling. In himself he was nothing.
  D. Speech—vv. 4-5
   1. Preaching—v. 4. There is no need for fancy words, just simplicity with the power of God. Note Philippians 4:13.
   2. Power—v. 5. Have faith in God, not faith in self, experiences or intelligence.

The same gospel that Paul preached should be preached today! The same gospel that changed man then will change man today! God has not changed; His power hasn't changed—Hebrews 13:8. There will be those who reject the gospel as they did with Paul. God gives the responsibility to Christians—preach the Word, and leave the results in His hands.

23

Paul Preaches at Ephesus

Acts 19:8–10; 20:17–21, 25–27

The city of Ephesus was filled with visitors and tourists. As with most large cities, there was much sin and ungodliness. Paul stayed in this city for three years. All seven churches of Revelation were started during this time. As Paul preached in this city revival broke out. The power of the Holy Spirit always brings God's power. It has been said, "Preaching of God's Word will make man mad or glad."

I. The Firm Ministry—19:8–10
A. Paul's plan—v. 8. He went into the synagogue and spoke boldly for three months.
B. Paul's problem—v. 9.
1. Stubborn people. They were hardened and refused to believe. Compare with Proverbs 29:1.
2. Sinful practices. They spoke evil of Paul's teaching, trying to discourage people from believing. See John 12:40.
3. Spiritual people. Paul took his followers and trained them. He wanted them to know what they believed and why—II Timothy 2:15. See also II Peter 3:15.
C. Paul's persistence—v. 10. Paul stays in this city two more years. The Greeks and Jews throughout all Asia hear the gospel.

II. The Faithful Ministry—20:17–21
A. Faithful pastor—v. 17. Paul called the elders together to give them final instructions, since they would carry on his work.
B. Faithful person—vv. 18–19. Paul was with these people for three years. He faced all kinds of problems, sorrows and suffering. See I Corinthians 15:30–32, II Corinthians 1:8–10. Note: (1) He served the Lord with humility of mind. (2) He shed many tears. (3) He faced many temptations. (4) He was threatened by the enemies of the gospel.
C. Faithful preaching—v. 20. He preached the full gospel; this met all the needs of the people.

48

III. The Final Ministry—20:25-27

A. Farewell—v. 25. Paul soon would leave and never see these people again. He was faithful to them throughout his ministry. Churches and all Christians enjoy many blessings because of the faithfulness of spiritual leaders.

B. Faithful—v. 26. Paul gave his very best. No one could accuse him of indifference. All Christians should read Ezekiel 3:18 often. This will drive them to win others to Christ.

C. Fullness—v. 27. Paul gave the full counsel of God. In other words, he preached the full gospel—Mark 16:15-18.

Paul preached what God told him to preach, which was the full gospel. He did not preach to please people. Note Paul's words to Timothy in II Timothy 4:2. In II Timothy 4:3, note these words: "For there is going to come a time when people won't listen to the truth, but will go around looking for teachers who will tell them just what they want to hear"—LB.

24

Paul's Arrest in Jerusalem

Acts 21:27–34, 37–40

Paul spent much time in prison and before judges and other authorities. Though it meant suffering and sorrow, he did not change his message. He could have remained silent, but his message meant more than anything that could be done to him. He was willing to stand for truth, even if it meant great suffering. He could say, "None of these things move me"—Acts 20:24.

I. **The Degradation of Paul—vv. 27–29**
   A. Agitation—v. 27. The people are incited by false reports. One agitator can stir up many problems among Christians and the church. He can do much damage to God's work.
   B. Attitude—v. 28. The people said the Jewish temple was defiled by bringing Greeks into it. Note the words of Peter: II Peter 3:9. Also see John 3:16.
   C. Association—v. 29. Trophimus was an Ephesian Christian— I Timothy 4:20. Paul brought Trophimus into the temple. Paul is accused of defiling the temple with this Christian brother.

II. **The Attempted Destruction of Paul—vv. 30–34**
   A. Persecution—v. 30. Paul was attacked by the people. He was whipped and mistreated as he was taken away. One may disagree with others' belief in God, but we are never to mistreat those who disagree with us.
   B. Punishment—v. 31. The people had one desire—to kill Paul. Narrow-minded people cannot think straight. Note the prophecy of Jesus—Matthew 24:9. Satan had one plan— destroy! These Jewish people allowed Satan to work through them.
   C. Protection—vv. 32–34. They stopped the whipping and placed Paul in chains. God used non-Christians to keep Paul from being hurt, and perhaps even killed.

III. **The Defense of Paul—vv. 37–40**
   A. Paul's plea—vv. 37–39. Paul speaks in Greek to the colonel. They thought he was an enemy seeking to destroy the govern-

ment. He wanted freedom to speak. Some people want freedom for themselves, but not for others.
B. Paul's preaching—v. 40. Paul speaks in the Hebrew. He tells
of his conversion. He was a Jew who had met Christ—Acts
9:1–20. He was changed from a persecutor to a preacher.

A football can be kicked many times, yet not break. The reason it
doesn't break is that the pressure on the inside is greater than the
pressure on the outside. Paul had something inside that was greater than
the problems, sufferings and sorrows on the outside. Note these words
in I John 4:4, ''. . . Greater is he [Jesus] that is in you, than he [Satan]
that is in the world.'' The more of God we have inside, the easier it will
be to withstand the things we face on the outside.

25

Paul Defends the Truth

Acts 22:1–30; 23:1–10

What is truth? Jesus said He was the truth—John 14:6. Jesus also said God's Word was truth—John 17:17. When man knows the truth he will be set free—John 8:32. Many don't want the truth, since it would set them free from sin. God's Word is a mirror showing man his sin. This is why Satan opposes the Bible. Because Paul stood for the truth he suffered much.

I. Defense of His Experience—22:1–21
A. Persecuting—vv. 1–5. Paul tells how he persecuted and killed Christians. See Acts 8:1–5; 9:1–20.
B. Power—vv. 6–11. Paul tells how God spoke to him and how he was blinded by the light from heaven. Paul, who was spiritually blind, is now physically blind. He tells how his life was changed by the power of God. See his words in II Corinthians 5:17.
C. Plan—vv. 12–16. Ananias, a devout Christian, prays for Paul and Paul is healed of his blindness. He is baptized and goes out to work for the Lord. Paul didn't wait; he immediately began to work for the Lord! He knew Mark 16:15 and John 15:16.
D. Prayer—vv. 17–21. Paul tells of a dream from God telling him to leave Jerusalem. He tells how he watched Stephen die and how God would send him to the Gentiles.

II. Defense of His Rights—22:22–30
A. Captured—vv. 22–24. Paul's preaching incited the people. They were people opposed to Christ. Jesus said, "And ye shall be hated of all men for my name's sake: but he that endureth to the end shall be saved."—Matthew 10:22.
B. Citizenship—vv. 25–28. Paul let the people know he was a Roman and that he had certain rights. We as Christians are citizens of heaven—John 1:12, Romans 8:17. We are citizens of two worlds.

III. Defense of His Faith—23:1–10

A. Punishment—vv. 1–3. The Jews attack Paul, hitting him and mistreating him. Paul tells them that God will take care of such people. Always remember Galatians 6:7–8. See also Matthew 5:10–12.

B. Prophecy—vv. 4–5. Paul didn't mean to speak against religious leaders. He knew the words of Exodus 22:28, "You shall not blaspheme God, nor curse government officials—your judges and your rulers."—LB.

C. Personality—v. 6. Paul explains that he is a Jew and believes in the resurrection. He says these people are not fighting over him, but over the fact of the resurrection.

D. Problem—7–10. The Sadducees didn't believe in the resurrection, angels or spirits, while the Pharisees did. God protected Paul—v. 10.

Paul knew Christ in a real way; he met Christ in a personal way. He had great faith in Christ—II Timothy 1:12. This faith caused him to be mistreated and to suffer more than any other man in the Bible. If he had not told the truth he could have been free. To Paul truth meant more than being free. Always stand for the truth!

26

Paul Escapes Death

Acts 23:11-35

The life of Paul was saved because someone was willing to "get involved." So many today have the "don't care" attitude. Paul's nephew, who many feel was not a Christian, risked his life to save Paul. As Christians we should stand for what's right. We should stand for: (1) the church, (2) the truth, (3) the Lord, (4) the pastor, (5) fellow Christians. God's work often suffers because some Christians are not willing to get involved. These same people will listen to gossip, criticism and complaints against God, the church and the pastor.

I. The Resolution of the Plan—vv. 11-15
   A. Promise—v. 11. God appears to Paul, assuring him not to be afraid, and tells him that he will preach in Rome. God will not desert us—Matthew 28:20, Hebrews 13:5.
   B. Pledge—v. 12. The people pledged not to eat until they had killed Paul. Their hatred turned them to murder. It started with Cain many years ago—Genesis 4:1-8. These were religious people!
   C. People—v. 13. There were forty men. Some were strict, religious Jewish people, yet they wanted to kill.
   D. Plea—vv. 14-15. The people asked the captain (commander of 600-1,000 men) to bring Paul out to be killed. They didn't hate Paul when he was a sinner.

II. The Revealing of the Plan—vv. 16-22
   A. Hearing—v. 16. Paul's nephew (no name given) heard of the plan. He goes to Paul and tells him of the plan. Christians should be concerned about others—Galatians 6:1-2.
   B. Help—vv. 17-22. The nephew endangered his life to help Paul. This love for Paul should be the same love in all Christians.
   C. Hazard—Acts 15:26. All the great men of the Bible risked their lives for the Lord. Moses, the prophets, the disciples, the church fathers all suffered greatly. Jesus spoke of being persecuted—Matthew 5:10-12.

III. The Release from the Plan—vv. 23–35

   A. The escape—vv. 23–24. The captain calls for 200 soldiers as a guard to take Paul to Caesarea to appear before Felix. God does protect His people—Psalm 91:1, 4, 11–12.

   B. The explanation—vv. 25–30

      1. Plan—vv. 25–27. The letter to Felix explains how the people were ready to kill Paul and the captain protected him.

      2. Purpose—vv. 28–30. Paul spoke to the Jews, telling them how they rejected God's laws. This caused anger and hatred.

      3. Protection—vv. 31–35. God's hand remained upon Paul. We may face death, but God is with us—Psalm 23:4.

God's work suffers because of indifference on the part of Christians. Some "Christians" are not willing to stand for what is right. Slowly evil overcomes the good because so few oppose evil. We should always stand for what is right, even if it means suffering. Jesus said we should not fear those who can harm the body, but fear the one (Satan) who can both destroy the body and soul—Matthew 10:28.

27

Paul's Defense Before Felix

Acts 24:1–27

The apostle Paul defended the gospel—Philippians 1:17. He was willing to stand for what was right, even if it meant standing alone. Paul did not defend himself—he defended the gospel. If standing for the truth meant death, Paul was willing to die—Phillipians 1:19–21. When people are as dedicated to God's work as Paul was, it offends and disturbs the non-Christian. If we defend God's Word, God will defend us!

I. **False Accusation—vv. 1–9**
   A. People—vv. 1–2. Ananias is a high priest. Tertulus is an expert in court and the law. Tertulus explains to Felix the charges that the Jews had brought against Paul.
   B. Praise—vv. 3–4. Tertulus uses flattery with Felix. In doing this he gets attention and respect. Too much flattery can be a form of lying.
   C. Problem—vv. 5–6. Paul is accused of defiling the temple by allowing the Gentiles to come and worship God.
   D. Protection—vv. 7–8. The captain saves Paul's life by bringing him to Felix.
   E. Politics—v. 9. The Jews, wanting to please Felix and the other leaders, lie to agree with the charges by Tertulus.

II. **Fearless Attitude—vv. 10–21**
   A. Proof of worship—vv. 10–13. Paul could prove that he didn't argue or make trouble. He wanted only to please God. See Philippians 3:10.
   B. Plan of worship—vv. 14–16. Paul worshiped Christ according to the Scriptures. He believed that all people would rise from the dead—Daniel 12:2. Both Christian and non-Christian would rise. See the plan for Christians to rise from the dead—I Thessalonians 4:13–18. For the sinner's resurrection, see Revelation 20:11–15.
   C. Practical worship—vv. 17–21. Paul brings money from Jerusalem to the Christians. There was no fighting; there were

no problems. The Jews had lied. Note Jesus' words in Matthew 5:10–12. Note two things: (1) persecuted for righteousness sake, (2) saying all manner of evil against us falsely for His sake.

III. Faithful Attention—vv. 22–27

  A. Freedom—vv. 22–23. Paul was freed on bail for a short time.
  B. Profit—vv. 24–26. Felix kept sending for Paul to come and see him. In verse 26, we see how Felix was expecting money from him in the form of a bribe.
  C. Politics—v. 27. Felix kept Paul in prison to please the people. If Paul would have given him a bribe he could have been free.

When one stands for the Scriptures some church people will oppose it. Some churches give little if any Scripture to the people. When a church preaches God's Word it is often called narrow-minded or old-fashioned. Paul warns that in the last day people will want to hear preaching that they enjoy—not the preaching they need (II Timothy 4:3).

28

Paul Before Agrippa

Acts 25:1-27, Acts 26:1-32

Paul defends himself before Agrippa. As the result Agrippa hears the gospel. Later, Paul tells how all things in the Christian life are for good—Romans 8:28. Joseph was sold as a slave into Egypt. He didn't understand why, but God had a plan for him. God had a job for him. Your problems, sorrows, troubles and setbacks are all for a reason. Had Paul not been arrested, perhaps Agrippa, Felix, Festus and others would never have heard the gospel.

I. **The Wrong—25:1-27**
   A. Politics—vv. 1-5. Festus wants the Jews to agree with him that Paul was guilty as charged.
   B. Proof—vv. 6-8. Paul proves before Felix that he did no wrong. Paul did nothing against the Jews or God's law.
   C. Persuasion—vv. 9-12. Festus tries to persuade Paul to admit he is guilty. However, Paul did no wrong.
   D. Procrastination—vv. 13-23. Festus didn't want to face the issue; he wanted to put it off—Isaiah 55:6, Proverbs 27:1.
   E. Problems—vv. 24-27. How could they convict Paul? All of the charges were lies.

II. **The Witness—26:1-23**
   A. Request—vv. 1-3. Paul requests that the people listen to him.
   B. Religious—vv. 4-5. Paul was religious and kept the Jewish law. He was religious, but not righteous! There is a difference!
   C. Resurrection—vv. 6-8. They refused to accept the fact of the resurrection. See Daniel 12:2, I Thessalonians 4:13-18, Revelation 20:11-15.
   D. Rejection—vv. 9-11. Paul was religious, yet he killed the Christians. He was blinded to the truth—II Corinthians 4:4.
   E. Redemption—vv. 12-18. Paul meets Christ and his life is changed. See his testimony in II Corinthians 5:17.
   F. Repentance—vv. 19-20. Paul preaches repentance. See II Peter 3:9.

G. Reminder—vv. 21–23. Paul reminds them of the Old Testament prophecy. See II Peter 1:21.

III. The Working—26:24–32

A. Conviction—v. 24. Paul's speaking brought conviction; God's Word brings conviction—Heb. 4:12. He is also accused of being crazy.

B. Confirmation—vv. 25–27. What Paul said was true; he had proof.

C. Convinced—v. 28. Paul almost persuaded Agrippa to become a Christian. Almost is not enough! See Isaiah 55:6.

D. Concern—v. 29. Paul wanted Agrippa to become a Christian *now!*

E. Complete—v. 30. The trial is complete and Paul is set free.

Agrippa had an opportunity to accept Christ, but rejected Him. We don't know if he ever had another opportunity. God's Spirit does not always strive with man—Genesis 6:3. When God speaks we better obey. If we harden our hearts God may cut us off—Proverbs 29:1. God may tell us to witness as a Christian.

29

Faith in a Storm

Acts 27:1–44

Paul had great faith in God. In this passage we see his faith in action. All Christians should read the eleventh chapter of Hebrews and study the great men of faith as they are pictured in this chapter. God wants all people to have faith. Unless we have faith we cannot please Him— Hebrews 11:6. What is faith? Faith is, simply, believing before you see—Hebrews 11:1. As you read Scripture your faith will increase— Romans 10:17.

I. The Plan—vv. 1–13
  A. Detained—vv. 1–3. Paul and other prisoners were put into chains and taken to Italy. Julius, a captain in Caesar's army was responsible for Paul and the prisoners.
  B. Danger—vv. 4–8. A storm comes. In the Christian life there will be problems. "Many are the afflictions of the righteous: but the Lord delivereth him out of them all"—Psalm 34:19.
  C. Disobedience—vv. 9–13
    1. Suggestion—vv. 9–10. Paul suggests they lighten the ship to keep it from sinking.
    2. Stubborn—vv. 11–13. They refuse to listen to Paul's advice. The world would be a better place to live if people would listen to the Christians.

II. The Problem—vv. 14–20
  A. Trouble—vv. 14–17. A bad storm comes and there appears to be no hope. They throw out many of the things on board to lighten the ship. Paul said all things were counted as loss— Philippians 3:7–8.
  B. Testing—vv. 18–20. Days pass and they don't see the sun or stars. They are lost. Christians will face storms in their lives:
    1. Storm of sickness—it will come to all people.
    2. Storm of sorrow—all must face this from time to time.
    3. Storm of suffering—Christians will be persecuted and misunderstood.

III. The Peace—vv. 21–44

A. Promise—vv. 21–26. Paul had faith that everything would be alright. All would be safe. See Hebrews 11:6.

B. Patience—vv. 27–32. After fourteen nights of storm they anchor the ship. All are told by Paul to remain on the ship.

C. Plan—vv. 33–35. For fourteen days they did not eat. Now, all 276 on the ship eat. Paul first prays and gives thanks to God for the safe keeping and for the food. See Romans 1:16, I Thessalonians 5:18.

D. Protection—vv. 36–44. The ship sticks in the sand. The leaders were going to kill the prisoners, but Paul orders them not to do it.

God creates faith—Satan destroys faith! Satan brings doubt, worry and mistrust. All Christians should have faith: (1) faith in God—never question or doubt Him, (2) faith in self—Philippians 4:13, (3) faith in others—always think the best of other Christians. Faith brings us near to Christ; it will help us live close to Him.

30

Paul's Ministry at Rome

Acts 28:1–31

Paul is in chains; he is a prisoner for preaching the gospel. Man may imprison our body, but not our soul. Though Paul's body was in chains he was free in the spirit. Though he spent much time in prison he knew real freedom in Christ. Today many are prisoners to (1) fear, (2) sin, (3) habits. Christ came to set man free. Freedom of the spirit is more important than freedom in the body.

I. The Supernatural—vv. 1–10
    A. Prisoners—vv. 1–2. Paul and the other prisoners arrive at the island of Malta. The people are very kind to him. Note Paul's words concerning kindness—Ephesians 4:32.
    B. Problem—vv. 3–4. A poisonous snake bites Paul. The people said he was a murderer, and God was punishing him. The Bible warns against such judgment—Matthew 7:1–5.
    C. Protection—vv. 5–6. Paul did not die from the snake bite. Note the promise of Jesus—Mark 16:18. When Paul didn't die from the poisonous snake the people said he was a god.
    D. Power—vv. 7–9. Paul has power as he prays for the sick. This is a fulfillment of Mark 16:17–18.
    E. Provision—v. 10. The people show their thanks and appreciation to Paul. Do you thank those who help you?

II. The Sincerity—vv. 11–23
    A. People—vv. 11–14. The people wanted Paul to stay. They were hungry for God. Note Paul's desire—Philippians 3:10.
    B. Praise—v. 15. People were there to greet Paul. They were not fearful of any persecution, and Paul thanked them for their courage. Are you ashamed of Christ? See Mark 8:38.
    C. Protection—v. 16. Paul was protected by God. He could have been destroyed, but God had work for Paul to do.
    D. Prisoner—vv. 17–20. Paul says he is in chains because he believes Christ is the Messiah. They could find no wrong in him.

E. Preaching—vv. 21–23. They had heard nothing wrong about Paul. They knew all Christians were persecuted—II Timothy 3:12. Note verse 23—Paul speaks from morning till night. See II Timothy 2:15.

III. **The Salvation—vv. 24–31**
   A. People—v. 24. Some believed and some didn't.
   B. Prophecy—vv. 25–27. Prophecy from Isaiah 6:9–10. (1) They hear, but don't understand. (2) They see, but are closed to the truth. (3) Their hearts are hard.
   C. Plan—v. 28. Salvation is for Gentiles, as well as Jews. See Romans 1:16.
   D. Preaching—vv. 29–31. The Jews were confused. Paul remained here for two years preaching the gospel.

Paul's life as outlined in the Book of Acts can be summed up in this way: (1) He persecuted and killed Christians. (2) He met Christ and his life was changed. (3) He suffered greatly under the persecution of Jewish leaders—but with supreme patience. (4) His preaching was simple and powerful. (5) He obtained great power with God and man. (6) Paul was persistent; he never gave up the work of the Lord.